RUSHDEN IN THE 1970s

Peter Butler was born in Podington in 1934. He was educated at various schools in Portsmouth during the early years of the war, followed by two years at Oban High School and finally at Harrold County Secondary Modern.

In 1949 he became apprenticed to Geoff Morgan, the electrical engineers in Church Street, Rushden. In later years he was attracted to the then new world of electronics and returned to Wellingborough Technical College to study radio and television servicing.

For two years in the late 60s he changed roles with his wife Lilian so that she could return to full-time teaching and he could look after their two children. After this period he returned to television servicing.

In 1974, whilst working for the Co-op in Wellingborough, he was faced with having to travel to Northampton to the new workshops there. This did not appeal, so he took a job, 'for a fortnight', with Unilever Research at Sharnbrook. Those two weeks extended to nearly 21 years, and during this time he worked exclusively in food research.

Peter has lived in Rushden since 1959 and has been photographing the changes taking place in the town for many years. The opportunity for early retirement at the end of 1994 enabled him to concentrate more on his various interests, which include railways, mountaineering and his membership of the Methodist church.

RUSHDEN IN THE 1970s
One man's photographs, memories and thoughts

PETER BUTLER

W.D. WHARTON
Wellingborough

First published in 1996 by
W.D. Wharton
37 Sheep Street
Wellingborough
Northamptonshire NN8 1BX

ISBN 1 899597 03 4

Designed and typeset by John Hardaker, Wollaston, Northamptonshire
Printed and bound in Great Britain by
Stanley L. Hunt (Printers) Ltd., Midland Road, Rushden

CONTENTS

INTRODUCTION

Rushden has been fortunate in recent years in that various people have not only been interested in the town's history, but been willing to compile and publish collections of their own, and other people's photographs.

The Rotary Club published an album in 1979 and, more recently, Eric Fowell has produced two more collections of his photographs of the early days of the town.

Over the last 25 years I have been photographing some of the changes that have taken place in Rushden. The interest shown has prompted me to produce this collection in the hope that memories will be stirred of people, places and things belonging to the not too distant past.

I ought to state quite clearly at the outset that I do not consider myself to be a professional photographer, only an amateur who has tried to keep a record of some of the changes. Since it has never been my main hobby, many buildings had been half demolished by the time I got there!

The photographs, memories, comments and thoughts are entirely my own. Doubtless I shall have some facts wrong. I shall be pleased to hear from anyone who can correct my errors.

P.E.B. Butler
Rushden
1996

ACKNOWLEDGEMENTS

Although, as I stress in the introduction, all the photographs were taken by me, when it came to writing about them I found that many queries arose which I could not answer.

I was always taught that if you don't know something for sure, go and ask someone who does! This I have done many times over recent months and I am glad to say that, without exception, everybody has been willing to help.

One person I owe a special debt to is Eric Fowell. He probably is the most knowledgeable person on Rushden's history and, as a result, got the largest share of my questions.

My thanks to Robert Wharton for being willing to publish this album. I hope his faith in me is justified. Finally, many thanks to my wife Lilian who has read, commented and corrected my writings and, of course, given me so much encouragement.

To all who have helped in any way, my most sincere thanks.

THE CO-OP MILKMAN

In recent years we have seen the decline in the delivery of our 'daily pintas'. In the 1970s much of this business in Rushden was in the hands of the Co-op which employed quite a number of men. Many will remember the depot in Newton Road and the sight of all the milk floats having their batteries recharged overnight. In those days the area covered was not just Rushden but out as far as Wymington, Podington and Riseley.

One of my uncles, the late Bill Hadley of Wymington, was a Co-op milkman for many years and would often recount some of his experiences, including struggling through the snows in order to reach the outlying villages.

When I lived at Wymington, our Co-op milkman was a character called Ray. He could never refuse any hospitality that was offered at Christmas, and in consequence had to be rescued on more than one occasion! This was, of course, before the advent of drink and drive laws.

My photograph, taken we think either in the late 1960s or early 1970s, is of another Co-op milkman, Bill Whiteman. Our daughter had made a card for him since he was just about to retire.

In the summer of 1995 the Co-op milk delivery service ceased in Rushden, the last part of the old Empire to go.

I wonder how many people still have some of the early R.I.C.S. milk checks?

LAURIE GREEN

Anyone who has ever walked in the Wymington Road area in the past will doubtless remember meeting little Laurie Green.

When I lived in Wymington in the late 1940s and early 1950s, Laurie lived in a converted barn on a farm at the bottom of the High Street in the village. He was a simple soul who loved the company of children. He would often walk to the bottom of Wymington Road in Rushden to meet the children off the bus after they had been to school in Bedford, and then carry their satchels back home for them.

Every Friday he would walk to the Co-op shop in High Street South with his little wooden box in which he would put his week's groceries. He always seemed to wear the same clothes, except on a Sunday when he would put his best suit on and his shiny boots and quite often walk into Rushden. He never had much material wealth, but I never recall hearing him complain in all the years that I knew him. When he died in 1977, some of what money he possessed was used to buy a new Pulpit Bible for the Parish Church at Wymington, whilst the remainder went towards the organ restoration fund.

My photograph was taken in 1972 when he had been shopping, but not with his box. In our conversation I asked him how old he was. He replied with a laugh 'I'm a hate and a ought,' which I interpreted as 80. All of us who knew him were poorer by his passing.

HIGH STREET SOUTH CO-OP

At the time of writing, all that is left of the Co-op in the town is the Funeral Service – very much a case of death having the last word!

For two years I worked for the Co-op in Wellingborough part-time and a further two years full-time. Here I was able to witness at first hand the kind of management that allowed things to drift to a point where the only option was to shut down the different departments. Having said that, I've always maintained that no one has ever lived life to the full unless they have worked for the Co-op.

At Rushden, the grocery and butchery shops in High Street South were amongst the first batch of closures. My photograph, taken in December 1979, shows that demolition had just started.

This was the shop my mother used, and I can still remember our 'divi' number. It's amazing how many people can still recall their Co-op dividend number. I remember being 'pressed into service' by my mother when she wanted something urgently. I would either walk or cycle from Wymington. Most young people today would surely be horrified if they were asked to walk three miles to buy some groceries.

HIGH STREET SOUTH

Another view (December 1979) showing the houses that were demolished at the same time as the Co-op shops. One wonders, with the benefit of hindsight, why such substantial houses had to be knocked down. It certainly wasn't so the road could be widened.

However, on the left-hand side of the road things remain unchanged. The most interesting thing that caught my eye was the sign outside Townsend's garage stating that the price of 4-star petrol was £1.23 a gallon. If we take the current price as being about 55 pence per litre and do the calculations, then the equivalent price for a gallon works out at £2.50. Think back to 1979 and how much your weekly wage packet was and then compare it with today's and I think that for most people the price of petrol today is cheaper than it was in 1979. But arithmetic was never my strong point and I have probably got my sums wrong!

JUBILEE PARK AND THE CO-OP

This sign is part of the gates leading into Jubilee Park from Bedford Road. I took the photograph in 1976, but it is still there for all to see today. It remains as one of the few pieces of evidence that the Co-op ever existed in Rushden.

It is difficult to believe that after the Second World War, when the Co-op was probably at its peak, it had over 20 shops and business premises throughout the town and district. Today the nearest grocery shop is in Higham Ferrers. When one looks at the new Co-op supermarket in Raunds, one cannot but wonder who or what allowed this situation to happen in Rushden.

Perhaps in the future some historian will think it worthwhile to do an in-depth study of this?

WHERE WAS IT?

In all the rest of this collection I've tried to explain where the various photographs were taken and when. This somewhat poor photograph of the back of a row of cottages was taken in December 1976.

Does anybody know where I was – there is a clue – or, better still, does anyone recognise their old back door?

No prizes, just something to get you thinking.

SOUTH END SCHOOL

Now for a few photographs with children as the main theme. I doubt if any of the youngsters will recognise themselves because I'm too far away. By standing in the middle of the A6 I could have gained a closer view but that was not to be recommended.

The date is July 1973 and the school is in its final days before transferring to the new school in Wymington Road. Looking at the picture you realise what a small playground it was, and made even smaller by the mobile classroom. Also there was not a single blade of grass for the children to see or play on.

I remember the days around 1971 when I used to take and collect our son to and from this school. Lilian and I had often talked about changing roles so that she could return to full-time teaching. In those days there were no problems in getting jobs for either of us.

So, for two years, I took the children to school, prepared the meals, did the washing, dusting, etc. Many people could just not come to terms with it – I must be at death's door – and treated me accordingly! My dear mother did not approve. It just wasn't done for a man who had got a job to deliberately choose to stay at home and do the housework.

What a comparison with today when many wives have to go to work either because their husbands are unemployed or it needs two incomes to remain solvent.

COUNCIL OF CHURCHES HOLIDAY CLUB

In the late 1960s and early 1970s, the Rushden Council of Churches ran some excellent holiday clubs for the youngsters of the town. This photograph and the following one were taken in 1971. How many children can recognise themselves I wonder? On the left is one of the 'regulars' at the holiday clubs. Cliff Pack was usually there together with his portable public address system. Sadly, Cliff died in the autumn of 1995.

One of the other projects that the Council of Churches ran – and still does – is the house-to-house collections for Christian Aid Week. At one time I was responsible for this and we had reached a stage when all the mainstream churches were involved. This meant we were in a position to cover every street in the town. One minister of a certain church, having agreed to be involved, would lock up all the envelopes and badges, etc. in his church's safe. This meant that when he wasn't there his people couldn't do the collection. On the third occasion this happened we made sure we had a spare set ready for the the faithful couple who wanted to do their share.

Since those days the Council has drifted apart. In 1995 only seven out of the 10 churches were willing to help with the collections, with the result that some areas of the town were not covered. I feel that there is a growing tendency for the churches to 'do their own thing'.

HOLIDAY CLUB

If you didn't recognise yourself in the first photograph I'm sure you will from this one. Incidentally, going back to that photograph, do you know who the two young ladies are holding up the sheet, or what was written on the sheet?

Well the words were:

> 'On the vict'ry side
> No foe can daunt me,
> No fear can haunt me,
> On the vict'ry side
>
> On the vict'ry side,
> With Christ within,
> The fight we'll win,
> On the vict'ry side.

Those words are as relevant today as they were in 1971.

In the background of this photograph is Rushden Hall. At about the same time as these holiday clubs were running, there was a public meeting called by the local Council to discuss the future of the Hall. One of the options was to demolish it. I remember asking at this meeting what do I say to my young son when he asks 'what was there Dad?'

Thankfully the meeting's wishes prevailed and our Hall still stands and is in regular use. Long may it remain so.

SPENCER PARK

Sometime in the early 1970s, this 'steam roller' was cemented into the ground by the children's swings. Where it came from I've no idea – perhaps someone can tell a bit more of its history from its number plate JT 9197.

Its popularity suggests it might not have been there very long. Our daughter, on the left, is not too sure about climbing aboard, whilst our son has no such reservations. He is the one climbing on to the roof!

Now, I must confess, I thought this 'climbing frame' would have disappeared years ago, but recently, when all the children were at school, I went to have a look. Most of it is still there. The roof and its supporting ironwork have all gone. A bit like Rushden, I thought, (and the author for that matter) – not all there any more!

Doubtless the decapitation was in the interest of safety. Naturally we should be concerned with our children's safety, but to me some aspects of safety have gone too far, and in so doing have deprived our youngsters of many of life's simpler adventures, and have prevented them from learning how to cope with the odd bump and grazed knee.

VIEWS FROM ST MARY'S

In 1972 the tower and spire of St Mary's was encased in scaffolding as a major programme of repair and maintenance was undertaken. Realising what a wonderful vantage point this would make, I sought out Les Priestley, who was Clerk of Works, and asked him if he would take me up the tower. This he was willing to do. My photographs were taken from just above the base of the spire which was as far as Les was prepared to let me go.

The first photograph looks out towards the old Lightstrung garage. Take time to look closely at the photograph and see how many changes you can spot. This location has for me special memories because it was at Geoff Morgan's shop (No. 28 Church Street, now Pizzeria Venezia) that I started my working life.

In the bottom left-hand corner stood Claridges shoe factory (now Stromag). Many of the factories in the town had diesel or gas engines for either driving the shafting or for generating their own electricity. Some actually did both. Claridges, if memory serves me right, had a marine diesel engine which stood resplendent in its tiled engine room.

Two doors up from Geoff's was Hart's Café. The wife of one of the town's boot and shoe manufacturers used to do the washing up here, not because, she would assure me, she needed the money but 'because I love washing up'. Her radiant smile would bear testimony to this statement and brighten the drab surroundings.

VIEWS FROM ST MARY'S

'Is it a bird? Is it an aeroplane?'

'No, it's your Father.'

My family gaze heavenward at the sight of their husband/father climbing around the scaffolding.

At this time Peter Crisp's emporium had not extended to Gramshaw's furniture shop or Jim Knight's hairdressing saloon. This latter establishment was a rather high class one and I cannot recall ever having my hair cut there. My barber was Lovell's in High Street South – now Barry Miller's. Lovell's had one attraction that Jim Knight's never had and that was his daughter; she used to cut hair! Quite unusual, I think, certainly for Rushden. I recall some of the young studs would be quite willing to change places in the queue in order to receive her ministrations. Ah happy days!

My main memory of Gramshaw's was that it specialised in the sale of prams. I'm sure there were other shops in the town that sold them, but for me the name Gramshaw and prams will always go together. I am reliably informed that we bought our pram there.

VIEWS FROM ST MARY'S

Of all the panoramas obtainable from St Mary's, this one must demonstrate, more than the others, the changes that have occurred to our town. All the John White factory complex has gone, whilst further up Newton Road the Co-op Dairy and Fish and Chip shop have disappeared, and on the opposite side of the road the row of cottages (Ebenezer Terrace) has been demolished.

I recall a dear old couple who lived in one of these cottages – a Mr and Mrs Eplett. They were from London, and when I visited them from time to time to repair their television they always seemed to be shouting and swearing at one another. Alf Garnett and his wife could easily have been modelled on this pair! Once I got to know them a little better I realised that this was just their way of life. They were, in fact, devoted to each other.

The United Counties bus garage was still open, but note how many cars there are compared to buses!

Just to the right of the centre of the photograph, in Park Road, is the building that once was the home of the old *Rushden Echo*. I remember going to do a job there and the operator of a Linotype machine asking me what my name was. When I told him, he set it for me in a slug of metal type. That was how typesetting was done in those days, and it makes one realise just what huge advances in technology have been made in a quarter of a century.

ST MARY'S DATE-STONE

I've deliberately included this photograph because it serves as a very timely reminder of the length of time the church has stood here. St Mary's dates from the thirteenth century, but when the restoration work was done in the 1970s, research undertaken then concluded that the origins of the structure could go back another century.

What is known for certain are these three dates – 1620, 1698 and 1718 when pointing work was done on the tower or spire. I took this photograph looking out from the top of the main tower, at a point where the spire commences. I wonder how many more date-stones there are like this around the church?

There can be no doubt that the gospel that has been preached in this church over the centuries is still as relevant now as it was in the twelfth and thirteenth centuries.

WINTER

Let me say at the outset that I enjoy winter weather; not your cold, dark damp and miserable Novembers, but those cold frosty days with, perhaps, some firm crunchy snow underfoot.

In February 1979 we had some 'lovely' weather, i.e. a grand blizzard! A neighbour and friend was a local GP and I had said to him that if we ever did have any bad weather and he needed to go out at night to visit his patients, I'd be quite willing to go with him and drive his trusty old Land Rover.

On 15 February we had had heavy snow for much of the day and there was no sign of things improving as evening approached. By 8 pm Rushden was virtually cut off. A call came from my friend Peter saying that he needed to go to see a pregnant woman who suspected that her baby was on the way! So off we drove through the snow. We got as far as the very deserted High Street and I had to stop to try to clear the windscreen of snow. Suddenly a door opened between two shops and out came several ladies who immediately told us everything was OK. Coffee and soup were ready and there were beds available!

The WRVS were up and running ready to help stranded motorists. I'm afraid we disappointed them when we told them what our mission was and that we were literally only a stone's throw from home. It was quite an evening for me, first trying to convince the father-to-be that everything was under control, before going on to Higham to bring the midwife and then ploughing our way to Wymington to make sure an elderly patient was all right.

My photograph was taken in the High Street with the WRVS offices on the right-hand side.

WINTER – WALKING TO WORK

Overnight, things had not improved much. It had stopped snowing but Rushden was still cut off, certainly from the south. I decided to walk to work at Sharnbrook. So, wearing my old faithful duffel coat and carrying my camera, I set off.

The police had closed the A6 in Bedford Road to prevent motorists from attempting to get through. The line of abandoned vehicles in High Street South at the bottom of Wymington Road shows the state of affairs. Up by the Rugby Club it was a mess. The east wind was blowing hard and the drifts were several feet deep. Quite a number of vehicles had been abandoned here and I had a bit of a problem getting round them.

At Avenue Road I ran out of film – typical – and looked for somewhere to shelter whilst I loaded a new one. Something was moving, and incredibly it was the good old Co-op milk float! How long the milkman had been on his rounds or whether he ever got home that day I shall never know, but I was able to crouch in the lee of his float long enough to change films.

Once I got past the last houses in Bedford Road the east wind really made its presence felt and was driving the snow off the fields horizontally.

WINTER – BENCROFT GRANGE

By the time I reached 'Bencroft Grange' I found myself in what is known as 'white out' conditions. So much snow was being driven off the fields that visibility was only a few yards – or metres – whichever you prefer. I got past the farm, turned round and tried a shot, knowing full well that conditions like this are rare indeed, especially in this part of the country.

What I didn't realise at the time was that the worst was almost over. I struggled on and as I neared Souldrop Turn the wood on the left protected me from the cold wind and the driving snow. As a result I felt much warmer.

WINTER – SOULDROP TURN

I realise I've come out of Rushden but trust you – the reader – will forgive me. As I approached Souldrop Turn there were only two vehicles in sight. It was the lorry that caught my eye! What was a lorry from Argyll doing there and what sort of fish was carried in an open lorry? What ever sort it was it was certainly of the frozen variety.

For me the worst part of the journey was over, and an hour later I arrived at work. I discovered that once south of Sharnbrook conditions were much easier, and most of the staff from the Bedford area had got to work. At least it meant the restaurant was open and I could get a hot meal.

I subsequently discovered that I was one of the few from the Rushden/Wellingborough area that had got to work that day and certainly the only one who walked. My Section Manager was very impressed and awarded me an extra three hours flexi-time, whilst the in-house magazine later spoke of my 'superhuman efforts'. Naturally my colleagues thought and said that I was mad, and they were probably right, but I enjoyed every minute of it!

ICICLES

Just to make you feel really cold and miserable, how about this shot of some real icicles! The location is part of Knight and Lawrence's factory in Manton Road, in March 1979. The previous day's winter sunshine had been sufficiently warm to start thawing the snow. Then as darkness descended, the temperature dropped and the next day we had these wonderful icicles. Like so many buildings in Rushden, all this area has been swept away and, in this instance, a block of flats built on the site.

For older generations the sight of icicles hanging from gutters and the beautiful patterns that the frost made on our bedroom windows were all part of life during the winter months. Now, with our milder winters and centrally-heated homes, these sights are becoming increasingly rare.

IRCHESTER COUNTRY PARK

For many folk, especially the older generations, snow, cold and dark nights hold no attraction. Nevertheless, for the youngsters and the young at heart, a good snowfall can be a wonderful opportunity for some fun and games.

I realise I have strayed out of Rushden again, but this photograph of my family and friends in Irchester Country Park warranted inclusion. It was a memorable time for more than one reason. Three of us were on the big toboggan when we momentarily lost control of it and shot down the side of one of the steep cuttings and found ourselves heading for a tree! We all threw ourselves off and let our toboggan hit the tree on its own!

On the way home we thought it a good idea to stop and get fish and chips for tea. Could we keep them hot until we got home? 'Never fear,' said our driver, 'There's a convenient ledge on the top of the engine. We'll put them there.' What we didn't realise was just how hot it got, because when we got back we found the wrapping paper had started to char and the contents had a sort of burnt paper/petrol/oily flavour. Never mind, we all lived to tell the tale.

HIGH STREET

A view that is unlikely to be repeated is this shot taken through the remains of one of Lawrence's shop windows. Lawrence's was a ladies dress shop, so my memories are somewhat limited! I do know that whatever the name may have been over the window, to the older generation of Rushden folk, it was always known as Archie Koffman's. Who Archie was or when, I don't know, but I'm sure that someone out there will put me right in due course.

The building in the trees was the old Rectory, now part of 'The Cloisters', a residential home for the elderly.

The notice clearly fixes the date when the site was to be sold. Sadly the building that was subsequently built here now stands empty (June 1996), another victim of out-of-town shopping complexes.

HIGH STREET AND 'THE ATH'

Another view of the final days of Lawrence's shop. Towards the right is the entrance to the upper part of the building which was known as 'Cleaver's Chambers'. In earlier years the building had housed one of Rushden's many Boot and Shoe factories. Next down the High Street was Horace Wills, one of the town's radio, television and electrical dealers.

In the early days of my appenticeship with Geoff Morgan, he had hired me out to Horace Wills's who had the contract to re-light the dance hall at the Athletic Club in Newton Road. Somewhat apprehensively I cycled up to 'The Ath' and introduced myself. They had installed some new fancy coloured lights in the ceiling, which was quite a height, as I was soon to discover. When they had switched the lights on they only glowed dimly! Despite checking the wiring they couldn't find the fault. Would I go and check? I climbed up the ladder and poked about. Not only had they wired them all up with twisted flex – which was strictly against the rules – but they had wired them in series instead of parallel! The electrically minded folk among readers will quickly realise why everything just glowed.

After that it was just a question of a lot of ladder climbing to sort it all out. I was very glad that this was the only time I was loaned out, and also perhaps why I've never had much fear of going up ladders.

HIGH STREET

One could be forgiven for asking why I've included this photograph in the album when at first glance nothing has changed – or has it? There are three names over shop premises which once were very familiar in the town for many years, but are now just memories.

Curry's, Saxby's and Dunkley's the gents hairdresser. I have very happy memories of dear old Mr Dunkley. I had discovered his shop years ago and always enjoyed my visits to him. I maintain that I paid for the entertainment and the haircut was thrown in for good measure! His quick witty banter, his singing and the odd dance step around the chair. You always had to allow plenty of time when you went for a haircut because he often abandoned his clients to serve another customer in the shop. Having a mutual interest in railways I always had to listen to the accounts of his latest excursion. One of my regrets is that I never thought to photograph his cheery smile.

He was one of the declining number of folk that I label as being 'characters'. I feel that we are all that much poorer because of the passing of such wonderful people.

HIGH STREET

Only one of the business premises in this photograph (December 1979) is still trading today under its old name, and that is Foster's. When I first came to live and work in Rushden in the early 1950s I believe that Wilson's was the only estate agent. In those days people tended to live in a house for years, even – in quite a number of cases – for life. As time went by houses were increasingly seen as a way of making money, so more people changed houses and more estate agents moved into the town until the balloon burst in 1989. Other early estate agents in the town, I recall, were Reg Birtles in Queen Street and Graham Willey in the High Street.

Turning to Webb's, this was the gents outfitters that my father patronised and where I was first introduced to the manager, Mr Arthur Larkinson: a tall, quietly-spoken man with a slight stoop who always made you feel that he had all the time in the world, even if you had only gone in to buy a pair of socks. For much of his life he could be found on Sundays occupying the pulpit of one of the Methodist churches in the area. Arthur was a 'local preacher'. It was John Wesley, the founder of Methodism, who recognised that people in the pews could be called to preach and why today many of our small village Methodist churches are still open.

Past Foster's shop, Geoff Knight's the jewellers can be seen and then, just visible on the extreme right, 'Shoppers Paradise' where Rushden's first supermarket 'Fine Fare' was opened.

ARTHUR SANDERS LTD

One of the well-established builders in Rushden when I started work was Arthur Sanders. Much of the building work, both industrial and domestic in the town and neighbourhood was done by this company. On many occasions when I worked for Geoff Morgan I often found myself on jobs where Sanders's men would also be working. This was always a good opportunity to mix with other craftsmen and to learn some of their skills.

Sadly, like so many other businesses in the town, closure came in the 1970s. My photograph, which was taken in 1972, shows the same notice and details of the auction as the one for Lawrence's in the High Street.

The road junction to the left of the picture is that of Coffee Tavern Lane and Rectory Road. The site was bought by the Co-op and their new store erected here. Within 20 years that complex was to close, and today (June 1996) it stands empty – an example of the increasing rate of change that was taking place everywhere and not just in Rushden.

ACCIDENT

Any good photographer will tell you that you should always carry a camera with you because you never know what might be just around the corner. Well on this particular occasion I had mine with me and was able to get my version of events. It was the sign on the van that made me chuckle! Note the official police photographer facing me with his camera on a tripod complete with his black cloth.

I dare say that the two Police officers came from the Police Station in North Street. The photograph was taken in the Spring of 1973 when Rushden had a Police Station that was open far more than it is today, and when you still saw the 'bobby' walking his beat.

The old Foresters' Office has over the years been attacked by quite a number of vehicles. Sadly, in August 1995, this location was the scene of yet another accident which this time claimed the life of a young boy. Increasingly in recent years this stretch of road has become a race track, with the inevitable tragic results.

QUEEN STREET – RECTORY ROAD

1975, and another little bit of old Rushden was about to disappear. 'Laddercraft' had been there for many years. In fact, I am reliably informed, it was there during the Second World War. Its speciality was invisible mending and I can well imagine that when ladies' stockings were in short supply there was a constant demand for what was a highly skilled craft. In its final days it had been taken over by Abingdon's the tailors in the High Street.

Moving down Rectory Road we come to the little cobbler's shop run by a Mr Shortland. One of the outcomes of the way footwear is made today is the disappearance of these small boot and shoe repair shops which, at one time, could be found all over our towns and cities. How many were there in Rushden I wonder?

When I came to look closely at the photograph, I didn't realise for how long the car park had been there. This must have been one of the first of Rushden's new car parks. People with long memories will know that this was the site of a row of old cottages known as Orchard Place. I'm not sure what day of the week it was when I took the photograph but note how few cars are visible.

FLOODS

In 1973 the railway bridge over the High Street was removed. Five years later, in May 1978, in an attempt to widen the road slightly, the station side bridge abutment and part of the embankment were removed.

Of course, in the 1970s we still had 'traditional' summers – in other words it rained! Looking back at the notes I made at that time, I see that it had rained almost non-stop for the previous 24 hours.

Since I knew the work was taking place, I'd gone to have a look and taken my camera with me, which was just as well, since it enabled me to get this photograph of the car trying to aquaplane up Station Approach!

On the extreme left of the picture is the old Birch Bros. garage, then in use by Hamblin's. Note the sign outside the hotel giving its original title, the 'Queen Victoria Hotel'.

STATION APPROACH

The year is 1973 and all the old station, which had not seen a train since 1969, is still standing and unvandalised. Parts of it had been let out to small businesses by the railway authorities and it was not until the mid 1970s that the Council took over the station goods shed and yard.

As most people will know, in 1985 the Rushden Historical Transport Society began renting the station from the Council and have developed a museum here in the intervening years.

The small tower appearing to sit on the fence at the left of the picture is atop of what were the stables of the old 'Queen Victoria Hotel'. The stables have since been demolished in order to make way for a small car park next to a new block of flats.

The position where the van is parked outside the front of the station is where the Eastern National Bus Company's service from Bedford stopped and started from. Whether this view will change/disappear with the proposed spur road from the bypass remains to be seen.

In June 1996 there were two developments which could result in increased interest in the area. First, a start was made in re-laying the track towards Higham Ferrers. Second, there was a proposal to build a Retail Park on derelict land at Skew Bridge and for this to be connected to the town by a new railway, using the trackbed of the original Wellingborough to Rushden and Higham Ferrers line.

The problems and costs involved will probably preclude the building of a new overbridge to cross the High Street, in which case the line would terminate at the back of Freeman's Garage.

HIGH STREET SOUTH

In 1972 at the site of what is now the BP petrol station stood three buildings. Nearest the entrance to the Hall Park was a building that reflected the current architectural style of the pre-war years. This building was used, I think, for most of its days as a ladies hairdressing salon. In earlier days it traded as 'Helene', whilst at the time of demolition it was called 'She'.

To the right of this shop and slightly set back was Robinson's garage. As I said in the introduction, so often by the time I had got round to doing any photography, demolition had usually started. In 1972 I was working for Wellingborough Co-op in the television service department and there wasn't a great deal of spare time for my hobby.

However, I'm sure this photograph will evoke a few memories from the ladies who had their perms here, and for the occupants of the flat above.

THE BLACKSMITHS

Continuing on from the previous photograph we come to Ginns & Son, the blacksmiths. This site, together with the old cottages that stood between Ginns's and what is now Edmund Chan's, the dentist, were also due for demolition. Whilst the ladies went to the first building, it was almost a male preserve at the blacksmiths. I do recall seeing young ladies there with horses to be shod but it was the exception rather than the rule.

Mr Ginns, if memory serves me right, was a short man who wore small round glasses. It was the man who took over the business, John, who I remember more clearly. It was to him we went when we wanted something making that we couldn't do ourselves, or when we wanted the odd nut and bolt or piece of metal. He was always helpful and willing to help us if he could.

I suspect that many of the work practices that John used would be frowned upon or banned by the current Health and Safety Regulations.

THE RUSHDEN ADULT SCHOOLS

It was whilst on my way to visit my parents, who lived just a little further along Wellingborough Road at No. 28, that I happened to spot the right-hand notice board which was announcing a 'Farewell Meeting'. This was in May of 1972.

In times past, many of our working class people had improved their education through such organisations as the Adult Schools. Their 'mission statement', to use the modern jargon, was painted on the left-hand board and read as follows:

> "ADULT SCHOOLS ARE GROUPS
> WHICH SEEK ON THE BASIS OF
> FELLOWSHIP TO LEARN TOGETHER
> AND TO ENRICH LIFE THROUGH
> STUDY, APPRECIATION, SOCIAL
> SERVICE AND OBEDIENCE
> TO A RELIGIOUS IDEAL."

Despite this high sounding ideal, my only memory consists of simply going there to mend the slot machines that controlled the lights over the snooker tables! Now the site has disappeared under another block of flats.

Whilst the Adult Schools may only be just another memory in Rushden, the organisation is still very much 'up and running' and you have to go no further than Higham Ferrers to find the nearest branch.

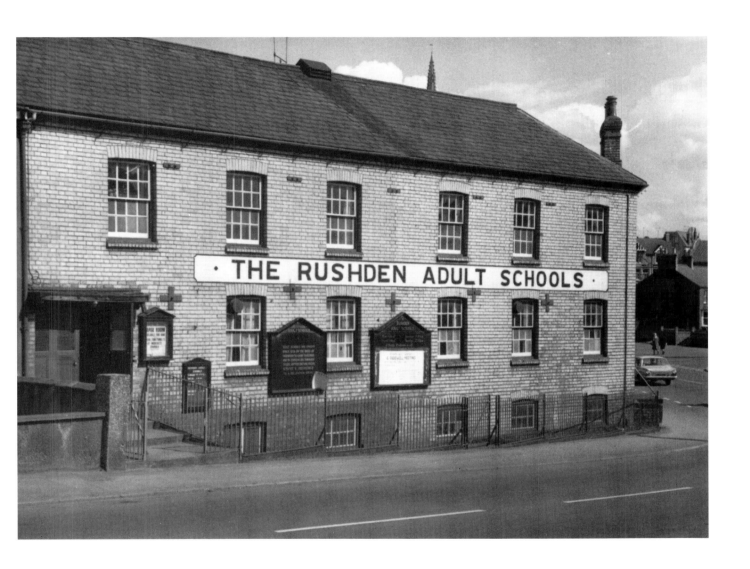

VIEW FROM THE TRAIN

Well not really, but it was a view that could have been seen in the days of the 'Higham Flyer'. In the summer of 1979 a new flood-prevention scheme was under way. The stream that flows through the grounds of Rushden Hall is carried on by a culvert that emerges by the side of Spencer Park. The work included slicing through the old railway embankment, part of which can be seen in the bottom right hand corner of the photograph.

Today the only thing missing is the factory of Jacques & Clark's which is in the centre of the picture.

My work with Geoff Morgan involved many hours spent in this factory and the one opposite in Station Road, B. Denton & Sons. In those days every factory had its own resident engineer. At Denton's it was Percy Cox, a somewhat rotund character with a wonderful sense of humour and always wearing his flat cap! Across the road at Jacques & Clark's the engineer was Billy Neal, a much quieter person, but one who I always felt reflected the more 'genteel' atmosphere in this factory compared to Denton's. I shall probably get told off about this comment, but I always felt the ambience at Jacques & Clark's was due in no small part to the Chapel-going habits of the management.

Today the Ambulance Station, like the Police Station, is only a shadow of its former self. The old BU building (The British United Shoe Machinery Co Ltd) is now the home of Hunt's the printers, whilst only Cyril Freeman's workshops are still in the same use as when the photograph was taken.

EATON'S IN COLLEGE STREET

This photograph was taken in March 1973. Now all that is left of another Rushden shoe factory are photographs and memories. When the children at Alfred Street School watched its demolition they told their teacher that they thought the machines clawing the building to pieces looked like monsters! The site is currently occupied by Budgen's Supermarket.

I'm sure the little telephone box built into the wall of the Post Office building will bring back a few memories to some folk. On a wet dark night it was a convenient spot for a quick cuddle, but a bit of a bind when someone wanted to use the booth for its intended purpose!

Although the adjacent Post Office building still stands, the public side of its business has been transferred into the supermarket, where the queues can be longer than they were in the old Post Office. I wonder what would happen if the supermarket were to close?

R. W. MUMFORD'S CLOSING ROOM

When the boot and shoe industry was in its infancy, the work was done in the workers' homes. As demand increased, not only did more mechanisation start appearing, but these machines were being grouped together in purpose-built factories.

One sector of the industry that still retained something of the early days, was the closing of the uppers. This work was done, almost exclusively, by the ladies. Although, when I got to know the industry, most factories had their own closing rooms on the premises, there were still quite a number of people who had a sewing machine in a shed at the bottom of the garden or in a spare bedroom. Sometimes they got together and used a small building in which perhaps six to twelve ladies would work together.

R.W. Mumford's was one of these and it was situated roughly where Peter Crisp's hardware department is today. It was on a piece of ground next door to Jim Knight's hairdressing salon. Being a shy sort of lad, I always entered this type of premises with a certain amount of trepidation. One or two of the ladies could embarrass a young boy!

One of the operations was called 'skiving'. It would be difficult to find a job that was more inaccurate in its description. To see a real skiver at work was to see a real skill being demonstrated. Sadly, I suspect that any of these little workshops that exist today will have fallen foul of the modern Health and Safety rules. They may have been a bit basic at times, but they were usually places with a happy atmosphere.

DUCK STREET 1

This photograph and the following two were taken in 1978 and serve as another reminder of how some areas of the town have changed. Everything in this picture has gone. For newcomers to the area, I'm standing in Duck Street, a few yards from the present roundabout.

The old building on the left had been used by a Mr Cave, who was an electrician. The house on the right had been the home of Mr Sanders, the builder, and I'm not sure who the cat, seen sitting on the wall, belonged to! He or she was probably still around after everything else had been cleared.

It is easy to see what a narrow stretch of road it was at this point and I don't think it was one-way either. Would today's impatient motorists have been able to cope with this? I doubt it somehow.

DUCK STREET 2

Like the previous photograph, everything in this scene has gone, including the lorry which belonged to 'Cromwell Services'. I'm standing looking along towards the present roundabout at the junction of Wellingborough Road, Church Street and Skinners Hill. Where the old stone cottages stood is now partly under Duck Street and partly under the grass verge in front of the Housing Association flats.

There was another small row of cottages which stood at almost right angles to the ones in the picture. The end wall of these former cottages is just visible in the centre of the photograph. My parents' home at No. 28 Wellingborough Road was a small stone cottage. This has survived and is now a very attractive modernised home. What a pity something could not have been done with these cottages and certainly with the modern houses on the left.

Nothing must be allowed to stand in the way of the motor car.

DUCK STREET 3

One more look at Duck Street. In contrast to the two previous views, here everything still stands. The photograph dates from July 1979 when the flood prevention work was in full swing. Duck Street was closed completely and my photograph shows the state of affairs when the work was almost complete.

In one of the cottages on the right lived Teddie Chettle who, when I knew him, kept some stables at the back of the cottages. Over the stables Geoff Morgan had, for a number of years, his workshop. In the winter months heating was provided by a big coke-burning stove. In the early 1950s it was the apprentices' job to go with a van to the Gas Works in Shirley Road and buy as many sacks full of coke that we could get into the back of the van. We were also responsible for lighting this stove. It could be quite a performance especially on a cold wet Monday morning. There was more than one occasion when we filled the place full of smoke before we got this pig going, helped by liberal applications of paraffin!

Access to the workshop was up a wooden staircase on the outside of the building. Everything to be repaired or serviced had to go this way. There was a hoist for the larger items, like electric motors. It was in these workshops that I repaired my first radio. How well I remember those hot summer days and the delightful aroma that permeated up from the stables beneath!

UNITED COUNTIES BUS DEPOT

The United Counties Omnibus Co. has served Rushden for many years. At one time three separate companies worked into the town. The famous Birch Bros., whose old depot still stands at the junction of Higham Road and Shirley Road, the Eastern National Co. and 'the Counties' as they were often referred to.

Like much of our public transport systems, the decline in our local bus services was under way in the 1970s. My photograph dates from March 1978. One bus stands outside at the back of the garage, whilst sticking its nose out is one of the buses used on the London service. By this time the United Counties had bought out Birch's business.

I was very grateful to Birch's because in my courting days they got me to London on a Friday evening in sufficent time to catch the last train from Waterloo that connected with the last train of the day from Guildford to Cranleigh, where my fiancée lived. It was always a rush to get away from work in time to have some tea, change and catch the 5.15 pm to London. After some time the drivers would look out for me and stop outside 28 Wellingborough Road to pick me up. Now that was real service!

The sharp-eyed among you will see that the pump at the entrance to the garage has a notice propped up in front of it. It reads NO FUEL. The end was nigh! Note, too, the traffic light which the staff could operate to allow buses to leave the garage.

THE PALACE

As most people will know, 'The Palace' cinema was one of three in the town. The advent of television sounded the death knell for many cinemas throughout the country and all of our three eventually succumbed.

The difference with this cinema from most is that the projection room was downstairs. This meant that tall people coming in at the back could, and did, block the film, much to the annoyance of the audience. 'The Palace' was one of my favourite cinemas in the 1950s because it showed 'The Bowery Boys' series of films. I've yet to see these repeated on TV.

I'm not sure when 'The Palace' closed, but at the time when my photograph was taken, April 1979, it had stood empty for a number of years before being taken over by the appropriately named 'Palace Motors'. The owners, Mr and Mrs Wills, had the bottom turned into a car showroom and a flat constructed above.

In 1978 a new GP to the town lived in this flat and had spent some time sorting out all his new patients' notes. He carefully put all the discarded material in the dustbin ready for collection next morning. He awoke to find that a gale overnight had blown the dustbin over and given Alfred Street the appearance of a New York ticker-tape welcome! He recalls very vividly his efforts to recover the myriad pieces of paper. Now you know why paper shredders were invented.

'THE ROYAL THEATRE'

This view of 'The Theatre' was taken from the railway embankment in March 1973, before the overbridge was removed. I'm not sure when this cinema closed, but readers of my book, *Midland Railway – The Rushden & Higham Ferrers Branch* will know that in 1959 it was still there going strong, because I was at the cinema whilst the last passenger trains were running by outside.

In June 1977 a serious fire resulted in a large portion of the building being demolished. It's interesting to compare my photograph with the one on page 48 of Eric Fowell's album *A Pictorial View of Rushden*. See how many changes have occurred in the intervening 60 years.

Note the gradient post in the bottom right hand corner of my photograph, another reminder of the town's rail link with Wellingborough. The number on the arms refers to the distance in feet during which the line rises or falls one foot. So the lower the number on the post, the steeper the gradient. I'm sure you all wanted to know about this and understand it perfectly now!

STATION ROAD

Two buildings that have gone from Station Road are the St John Ambulance Rooms and the old swimming baths. The former were rendered unusable after an arson attack, and the baths went when the area was redeveloped, partly in readiness for the new Splash Pool complex and the inevitable car park.

The old baths were open-air and my first memory is of being brought here from my school in Harrold, together with my classmates, for swimming lessons. The teacher, all wrapped up, would walk round the edge of the pool telling us what to do, whilst we nearly drowned or died of exposure. I did not enjoy it. I'm one of those who subscribe to the view that people shouldn't go into the water until they can swim!

However, unlike me, there was a small band of 'he-men' who went to the baths every morning, winter and summer, for a quick dip before breakfast. Amongst this band was Geoff Morgan and, I think, a young Jim Bugby.

My photograph was taken in July 1979.

PUBLIC MEETINGS

Years ago I seem to remember we tended to have more public meetings which attracted large audiences. Two of these meetings are firmly fixed in my memory, though both are, admittedly, pre-1970s. The first was one called to discuss whether 'The Ritz' cinema should be allowed to show films on a Sunday. The main hall in Alfred Street School was packed and people were not afraid to stand up and state their case for and against the proposals.

Then there was the Labour Party rally at the Boys' School in Tennyson Road addressed by the late George Brown. Fortified by a little alcohol prior to the meeting, George really was a master at animating his audience, and Rushden was no exception!

My photograph (July 1974) was of another Labour Party rally held outside Rushden Hall and addressed by Barbara Castle. The poster on the front of the table reads 'BIGGEST EVER PENSION RISE'.

Of course, today, television brings into our homes all the big names of politics, yet when a public meeting was held in 1994 in Rushden to discuss the possibilities of restoring the old RUDC, a subject that a lot of the townsfolk claim to feel strongly about, only 50 could be bothered to attend.

I feel that there is more than a grain of truth in some of the expressions that are used today, such as 'couch potatoes' and 'apathy rules'.

THE TIN TABERNACLE

Most people I'm sure will remember the old 'Tin Tabernacle' that stood in the grounds of Jacques & Clark's factory. It's worth recalling what it was doing there.

I had over the years heard various tales about it, but it wasn't until I found a little book in a jumble sale that gave me the facts on this building. *Memoirs: Leaves from a Bandsman's Diary* by Ernest Panter and published in 1943, sets out the story of the Rushden Mission Band and how the Tin Tabernacle played an important role in the band's history. The building had been opened in 1895 as a daughter church of the Independent Wesleyan Chapel in the High Street. In those days many of the town's shoe manufacturers were of the Non-Conformist tradition, amongst them being George Denton, John Clark and John Clipson, all well-known names in the town.

In 1897, the bandsmen of the town's Salvation Army had a major difference of opinion with the Corps Officer as to how the money collected from carol playing sessions should be allocated. Such was the strength of feeling that the bandsmen felt obliged to resign from the Corps and to hand in their instruments. As the book puts it, they became 'conscientious objectors'. Spiritually homeless, the men visited different churches on Sundays. Their visit to the High Street church made the leaders of this church think long and hard. The outcome was an invitation to the bandsmen to join this church and for funds to be made available to enable new instruments to be bought for the men who were unable to afford their own. The plan was accepted and the men decided to make their new home in the little Tin Tabernacle.

This worked well and the band became known as the 'Rushden Independent Wesleyan Mission Band'. In due course this little 'Bethel' proved too small to cope with the ever increasing congregations, and a bigger church was sought. So in July 1901 the new 'Mission Church' in Wellingborough Road was opened and the congregation and band moved to it. So, a hundred years later, whilst the 'Tin Tabernacle' is but a memory, the tradition that started there still lives on today.

SUCCOTH BAPTIST CHAPEL

I hope the reader will forgive me for including this photograph which was taken just before the chapel was demolished in March 1969. Photographs of this building have been published before, but it was the date stone that intrigued me.

FOUNDED 1805.
ENLARGED 1825, REBUILT 1864.
AGAIN ENLARGED 1893.

All this arising from a minor doctrinal difference of opinion with the original Baptist cause in Little Street. The chapel suffered considerable damage as a result of the fire at Cave's factory which stood across the road in the High Street in July 1901.

I've spoken to more people about this chapel than I have about any other topic in this album. All I have been trying to find out is, when did it close for public worship? I now know that when it closed it only had five members and that it stood empty for many years. Someone suggested it was abandoned before the Second World War, but I find this difficult to believe.

Rushden's churches and chapels bear witness to some of the major national splits that have occurred within Christianity and also what can happen at a local level. Methodism emerged from the Church of England and later Booth broke with Methodism because he claimed '… Methodism has become too respectable.' This gave rise to the founding of The Salvation Army.

From the previous story we can see how the Mission Church was partly brought about by the split from the Salvation Army.

I wonder what the Founder of Christianity thinks about it all?

'STEPTOE AND SON'

Couldn't leave this one out. A reminder of when times were hard, and having recently set up home with my wife, Lilian, in York Road, I heard that there were some doors going begging in the town, so had borrowed Bob King's handcart to go and collect them.

My photograph shows my father and myself arriving triumphantly back at York Road. It's amazing what a difference it makes having a door at the entrance to a room!

Some of the older generation may remember my father from the days when he worked for the Co-op in Rushden. In his youth he had served an apprenticeship as a shipwright in Chatham Dockyard. The recession of the 1930s had brought him, with his family, to live in Podington. Here he met my mother-to-be who lived in Wymington.

The rest, as they say, is history.